DELTA PUBLIC LIBRARY
402 MAIN STREET
DELTA, OH 43515

AR:
PTS: X

WITHDRAWN

JUL 25 2016

Americans in the Holy Land

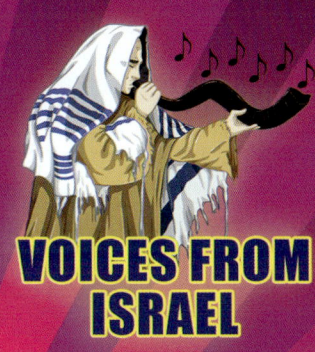

Voices from Israel

Gil Zohar

Mitchell Lane
PUBLISHERS
P.O. Box 196
Hockessin, Delaware 19707

Set 1
Benjamin Netanyahu

The Experience of Israel: Sights and Cities

I Am Israeli: The Children of Israel

Returning Home: Journeys to Israel

Working Together: Economy, Technology, and Careers in Israel

Set 2
Americans in the Holy Land

Culture, Customs, and Celebrations in Israel

Israel and the Arab World

Israel: Holy Land to Many

Israel: Stories of Conflict and Resolution, Love and Death

Delta Public Library

Copyright © 2016 by Mitchell Lane Publishers, Inc. All rights reserved. No part of this book may be reproduced without written permission from the publisher. Printed and bound in the United States of America.

Printing 1 2 3 4 5 6 7 8 9

Library of Congress Cataloging-in-Publication Data
Zohar, Gil, author.
 Americans in the Holy Land / by Gil Zohar.
   pages cm — (Voices from Israel)
 Includes bibliographical references and index.
 ISBN 978-1-61228-681-5 (library bound)
1. Americans—Israel—Juvenile literature. 2. Israel—Description and travel—Juvenile literature. I. Title.
 DS113.8.A4Z64 2015
 305.813'05694—dc23
                                                                                                2015017398
eBook ISBN: 978-1-16228-690-7

ABOUT THE COVER: Americans have been playing an important role in the Holy Land for centuries. Seen here clockwise from the upper left: basketball coach David Blatt, Henrietta Szold, Judah Magnes, Nobel Prize winner Robert John Aumann, and Prime Minister Golda Meir (center).

DEDICATION: Dedicated to my friend Yossi Birnbaum who immigrated to Israel from Oklahoma to serve in the Israel Defense Forces as a *chayil boded* (lone soldier).

    During the three-week-long Operation Cast Lead in 2009, when an Israeli infantry incursion sought to halt the incessant terrorist rocket fire from the Gaza Strip, Yossi telephoned me to say the next day he was "going south to Mexico." (Soldiers revealing their deployment are subject to court martial.) He then added that since he didn't have any relatives in Israel, he had listed my name to contact "if he didn't return alive from Mexico."
    Yossi's contribution—and that of all his fellow soldiers without family—represents the best spirit of Zionism and nation building.
    "He who watches over Israel neither slumbers nor sleeps."—Psalms 121:4

PUBLISHER'S NOTE: This book is based on the author's extensive work as a journalist based in Jerusalem, Israel. Documentation is contained on pp. 59–60.
    The Internet sites referenced herein were active as of the publication date. Due to the fleeting nature of some web sites, we cannot guarantee they will all be active when you are reading this book.
    To reflect current usage, we have chosen to use the secular era designations BCE ("before the common era") and CE ("of the common era") instead of the traditional designations BC ("before Christ") and AD (*anno Domini*, "in the year of the Lord").

PRONUNCIATION NOTE: The author has included pronunciations for many of the Hebrew words in this book. In these pronunciations, the letters "ch" are not pronounced like the "ch" in "children." Instead, the letters "ch" represent the Hebrew letter chet, which sounds like a "kh" or hard "h" sound, similar to the "ch" in "Loch Ness Monster."

PBP

CONTENTS

Introduction 6
CHAPTER 1: Explorers and Archaeologists 9
   American Schools in Israel and the Middle East 15
CHAPTER 2: America's Lost Colonies in the Holy Land 17
   Jerusalem's American Colony 23
CHAPTER 3: Visionaries and Crazy People 25
   Rabbi Shlomo Carlebach 31
CHAPTER 4: Philanthropists Who Shaped Israel 33
   Henrietta Szold—Founder of the
     Hadassah Women's Organization 35
CHAPTER 5: Politicians and Spies 37
   Jonathan Pollard—The Spy Who Embarrassed Two Countries 41
CHAPTER 6: Soldiers, Blockade Runners, and Gun Smugglers 43
   Smuggled Warplanes 45
**CHAPTER 7: SCHOLARS, BRAINIACS, AND ARTISTS—All With an
   American Accent** 47
   Woodstock Revival Offers a Heady Mix of 1960s Nostalgia 49
**CHAPTER 8: Hoopster Coach's Career from Boston to
   Tel Aviv to Cleveland** 51
   Baseball in the Holy Land 53

Chapter Notes 54
Works Consulted 59
Further Reading 60
On the Internet 60
Glossary 61
Index 63

Introduction

Like Europe's once mighty empires—Britain, France, Germany, Austria, Italy, and Russia—the United States built palatial monuments in Jerusalem in the late nineteenth century, competing for leadership as the Turkish Ottoman Empire tottered. Britain gained control of Israel, formerly known as Palestine, for nearly three decades beginning in 1920 until Israel gained its independence in 1948.[1] Of all these countries, it is the United States which has the deepest historic connection here.

Prior to America's declaration of independence in 1776, the thirteen colonies already had a symbolic connection to the Holy Land. The Puritans envisioned America as their Promised Land. The colonists mined the Hebrew Bible in naming places in their new country; hence names like Salem, Massachusetts (in the book of Genesis, shalem means peace), and Rehoboth Beach, Delaware (also found in Genesis). Yale University in New Haven, Connecticut, founded in 1716, inscribed in Hebrew *urim v'tumim* (light and perfection) on its seal, with the Latin words *Lux et Veritas* (light and truth). For the university's founders, these words were symbols of enlightenment.[2]

American explorers and archaeologists, colonists, visionaries, politicians, philanthropists, soldiers, spies, scholars, and athletes all played (or are still playing) a major role in Israel. There are an estimated 250,000 Israelis who also hold American citizenship. These people are examples of the relationship between Israel and the United States—an alliance based not only on mutual interests, but also on common values and a joint world-view. The two countries share democracy, liberty, human rights, the rule of law, entrepreneurship, and increasingly, a similar standard of living and way of life.[3]

Gil Zohar
Jerusalem

Jerusalem's Liberty Bell Park contains a replica of Philadelphia's Liberty Bell from which it gets its name. The nine-acre park, founded in 1976 to celebrate the US bicentennial, is one of the few places in Jerusalem where Jews and Arabs freely mingle.

In 1837 General Lewis Cass of the United States Navy dropped anchor off Jaffa planning to map the uncharted Jordan River and the Dead Sea—the lowest point on the face of the Earth. But the American sailors failed in their mission. Ill from sunstroke, they barely managed to return alive to their vessel the USS *Constitution*.

CHAPTER 1
Explorers and Archaeologists

In 1837 US General Lewis Cass dropped the anchor of the USS *Constitution* "Old Ironsides" off the coast of Jaffa, Palestine.[1]

Together with several US naval officers, Cass proceeded inland planning to survey the uncharted Dead Sea—the lowest point on the face of the Earth (over fourteen hundred feet below sea level), but the poorly equipped mission was a failure; ill from sunstroke, the sailors barely managed to return to their vessel alive.[2]

A decade later, Lieutenant William Francis Lynch of the US Navy led a better-provisioned sixteen-man expedition to explore the Jordan River and Dead Sea. Camels hauled the prefabricated boats specially manufactured of copper and galvanized iron overland from the Mediterranean Sea to Lake Kinneret. Lynch then proceeded down the meandering Jordan River, which is a creek by American standards. In tandem, a party proceeded on land. The mission mapped the Jordan's twenty-seven rapids and cascades. Though only sixty miles (one hundred kilometers) from Lake Kinneret to the Dead Sea, the river's winding course was two hundred miles (322 kilometers) long. Lynch described the Jordan as "more sinuous even than the Mississippi," clearly unsuitable for navigation.[3,4]

While advancing the cause of science Lynch was also at "the service of American commerce with the region." He reported "an extensive plain, luxuriant in vegetation, and

CHAPTER 1

The storied Jordan River of the Hebrew Bible and the New Testament is barely a creek by American standards. Inset: Every January Roman Catholic and Eastern Orthodox Christians come to Qasr al-Yahud—the traditional site where John the Baptist baptized Jesus in the Jordan River—to celebrate Epiphany.

presenting . . . a richness of alluvial soil, the produce of which, with proper agriculture, might nourish a vast population."[5] Indeed today many of the tomatoes, cucumbers, and other winter vegetables consumed in Europe are grown in the Jordan Valley.

While Congress shelved Lynch's report recommending colonization, it helped spark America's fascination with the Holy Land.

Numerous American writers went to Israel, including Hermann Melville, author of *Moby Dick*. His visit in 1856–1857 inspired his epic poem *Clarel: A Poem and Pilgrimage in the Holy Land*. Melville thought the Holy Land was a "pile of rocks," a "disappointment," and "a caked, depopulated hell." Ten years later Mark Twain visited the Holy Land and wrote about it in his travelogue *Innocents Abroad*, and he said, "Of all the lands there are for dismal scenery, I think Palestine must be the prince. Palestine is no more of this workday world. It is sacred to poetry and tradition—it is dream-land."[6,7,8]

Hermann Melville

American tourists pose in a cemetery outside of Jerusalem's walls, apparently outside of the Golden Gate, circa 1867. Mark Twain's extraordinarily popular travel guide *Innocents Abroad* inspired many Americans to visit the Holy Land.

Paradoxically Twain's description of the Holy Land's destitution inspired more nineteenth century American travelers including Ulysses S. Grant, who toured Palestine in 1878 shortly after leaving the White House. Grant was the first US president to visit Palestine.[9]

Reverend Eli Smith (1801–1857) of Northford, Connecticut was a remarkable missionary. Settling in Beirut (today the capital of Lebanon) in 1834, he began translating the Hebrew Bible into Arabic. Reverend Edward Robinson of Southington, Connecticut (1794–1863), known as the Father of Biblical Geography, joined Smith in 1838. The two missionaries set out

Explorers and Archaeologists

to explore Palestine's undiscovered and remote interior. Armed with the Bible written in English and Hebrew, the adventurers identified many ancient places. Among them were Hezekiah's Tunnel burrowed shortly before the Assyrian siege of Jerusalem in 701–702 BCE, and Robinson's Arch that led to King Herod the Great's Second Temple, which was begun in 19 BCE. (It was only after the massive excavations following the 1967 Six-Day War that archaeologists clarified that Robinson's Arch was part of a monumental stairway rather than a bridge to the Upper City, as the American explorer had believed.) Still, they named the stairway Robinson's Arch.[10,11]

Reverend Edward Robinson was an early explorer of Israel. Amongst his many discoveries was the remains of a monumental stairway, today called Robinson's Arch, which lead to King Herod's Second Temple that was destroyed by the Romans in 70 CE.

CHAPTER 1

Staring south through a telescope at the Ein Gedi oasis by the Dead Sea, Robinson and Smith identified Herod the Great's mountaintop fortress at Masada—where the last free Jews made their final stand in 73 CE in their desperate revolt against Rome. Their expedition led to the publication of *Biblical Researches in Palestine and Adjacent Countries* for which Robinson was awarded the Gold Medal of Britain's Royal Geographic Society in 1842.[12,13,14]

Like Robinson, William Foxwell Albright (1891–1971), who was born to Methodist missionary parents in Chile, had a passion for archaeology and the Bible. One of the developers of Jerusalem's American School of Oriental Research, he standardized pottery typology for the Holy Land—a breakthrough that allowed archaeologists to date finds from the same civilization in different mounds of ancient cities. Albright was able to establish that the Dead Sea Scrolls that had been discovered were genuine (1947–1948), and he established the Anchor Bible series of books that translated the Hebrew Bible and other related works. Robinson and Albright were the first of many American archaeologists to excavate in Palestine.[15,16]

William Albright excavated the biblical site of Tell Beit Mirsim from 1933 to 1936.

AMERICAN SCHOOLS IN ISRAEL AND THE MIDDLE EAST

Many nineteenth century American visitors were missionaries and educators. Among them was Sara J. Swift from an old Quaker family in Bedford, Massachusetts who in 1869 established the Friends Girls School in Ramallah, today the provisional capital of the Palestinian Authority. A boys school opened in 1901 in nearby al-Bireh. While the twin schools failed to convert many Muslims or Christians to the Quaker faith, they helped shape generations of Arab leaders.[17]

The US Embassy established the privately-operated Walworth Barbour American International School (WBAIS) in Israel near Tel Aviv in 1958; the school, today located nearer to Haifa, offers an American program that leads to a US high school diploma. The American School of Palestine, a co-ed institution established in 1995, provides a bilingual education for returning English-speaking expatriate Palestinian youth. The WBAIS operates a sister campus in Jerusalem.[18,19]

The Walworth Barbour American International School in Even Yehudah

Jerusalem's English-language University of the Holy Land, a Christian University, was founded in 1987, and offers masters-level and doctorate programs. Some Americans go to Israel to study medicine, and then return home to practice. Others spend months or years at *yeshivot* (seminaries) studying the Bible and Talmud (a collection of Jewish law and tradition) with English-speaking instructors.[20]

Reverend George Jones Adams founded the American Colony in Jaffa but was ill-prepared for farming in the arid Middle East.

CHAPTER 2
America's Lost Colonies in the Holy Land

New England in Tel Aviv—The American Colony at Jaffa

Known as the American Colony at Tel Aviv's seedy south end is a cluster of wooden clapboard buildings that look like they are straight out of New England.

The story begins shortly after the American Civil War. On August 11, 1866, one hundred and fifty-seven members of the Palestine Emigration Colony, including forty-eight children under the age of twelve, set sail from Jonesport, Maine for Jaffa on the newly-built, three-masted vessel *Nellie Chapin*.

George Jones Adams, leader of the thirty-five New England families, hoped to develop the Land of Israel in preparation for the biblically-prophesized return of the Jews. He believed it would hasten the second coming of the Christian Messiah. Adams had been a follower of the Mormon Church and he had quit the then newly established religion following the assassination of Mormon founder Joseph Smith in 1844. Most of the congregants of the Church of the Messiah he founded lived in Maine.

As they left the United States, Adams said, "We believe the time has come for Israel to gather home from their long dispersion to the land of their fathers. We are going [to Jaffa] to become practical benefactors of the land and people, to take the lead in developing its great resources." Their purpose was not to create a mission, but to assist the Jewish people in returning to Israel.[1,2]

CHAPTER 2

Though equipped with the latest agricultural tools, twenty-two prefabricated houses (manufactured houses in standardized sections that are ready for quick assembly), and religious fervor, the colonists' mission was doomed. Arriving in Jaffa, they learned that Adams had not yet purchased the land on which they planned to settle. Instead they pitched their tents on the beach near a cemetery where the victims of a recent cholera epidemic were buried. Within six months, twenty-two of the one hundred and fifty-seven settlers, including nine children, were dead.

Disease was not the settlers' only problem. After finally buying the property for their neighborhood, the first outside of Jaffa's Ottoman ramparts, the pioneers quickly learned that farming in the arid Middle East was nothing like agriculture in rainy New England.[3,4]

Children from Jerusalem's American Colony celebrating the 4th of July at the beginning of the 20th Century. Note the Statue of Liberty.

America's Lost Colonies in the Holy Land

Because the colonists were facing starvation and they continued to die, Adams turned to alcohol. Within two years after their arrival, all but two-dozen or so members of the American Colony had returned from Jaffa to America. Their buildings were sold to the newly arrived German evangelical Christians. Known as Templars, the Germans developed seven colonies across Palestine, until the British arrested them in 1939 as Nazi sympathizers. They were deported to Australia or sent back to the Third Reich in prisoner exchanges.[5]

Rolla Floyd (1832–1911), a pioneer of Israel's tourism business, was among the Americans who remained. In 1869 he opened the stagecoach service from Jaffa to Jerusalem on the newly paved road. The journey from the coast to the mountains took fourteen hours. A high-speed train due to be completed in 2018 will cover the same distance in thirty minutes.[6,7]

Rolla Floyd, a survivor of Jaffa's failed American Colony, became a transportation pioneer in Israel. In 1869 he established the stagecoach service from Jaffa to Jerusalem on the newly paved road. It was 1892 when a railroad opened along the same route. It was the first in the Middle East. Seen here is the Jerusalem Railroad Station circa 1900.

The Maine settlers were not forgotten thanks to Reed Holmes. In 1942, the historian met an elderly woman who had been thirteen when the *Nellie Chapin* dropped anchor. After four decades of research, Holmes published *The ForeRunners*. Around the same time, he organized a tour of Israel. Among the participants was Jean Carter, a licensed contractor from Massachusetts. Touring the former American Colony, she "was aghast" to learn that the decrepit, historic wooden houses were about to be torn down.[8,9]

Raised in a Protestant church, Carter had a master's degree in Jewish studies and was fluent in Hebrew. She persuaded the Israeli government to declare the former colony a heritage site, received a promise that any structure that could be preserved would be spared demolition, and she got the Tel Aviv Municipality to erect a plaque on the beach where the Maine colonists had landed.

America's Lost Colonies in the Holy Land

Holmes and Carter fell in love and eventually married. In 2002, they purchased Wentworth House, one of the remaining dilapidated American Colony houses. With the help of specialists in nineteenth century building preservation from Maine, the couple spent two years restoring the ruins and removing modern additions. Restored as the Maine Friendship House, the building houses a museum about Jaffa's American Colony.

The Holmes, who live in Jonesport, Maine were honored in 2004 by the Maine Preservation Society, the first time the society recognized a project outside of Maine.[10]

The restored Maine Friendship House in Tel Aviv is today a museum about the failed American colony in Jaffa. In 1869 the destitute Yankees sold their property to German evangelical Christians. Almost all returned to Maine.

Members of Jerusalem's American Colony established one of the first photo studios in the city. That archive, today housed in the US Library of Congress in Washington, DC, is an invaluable treasure about life in the Middle East in the late 19th and early 20th centuries. Seen here are Ottoman troops marching through Jerusalem's Jaffa Gate circa 1906.

JERUSALEM'S AMERICAN COLONY

Unrelated to Jaffa's American Colony is a Jerusalem settlement of the same name. Today it is a luxury hotel where foreign journalists like to belly up to the bar. Members of a Protestant utopian society led by Horatio Spafford of Chicago (1828–1888) founded the settlement in 1881 as a Jerusalem commune—Israel's first kibbutz.[11]

Spafford and his wife Anna, together with a group of fourteen adults and five children, expected Jesus' Second Coming. While waiting, the members of the settlement of Yankees and Scandinavians served the Holy City's many poor people by opening soup kitchens, hospitals, orphanages, and other charitable ventures.[12]

The charity was largely funded by the American Colony Photo Department. Many of those early images fall into the category of Orientalism, for which the West had a seemingly insatiable appetite. But part of that artistic achievement was due to good timing. The Colony's photographers began operating at a time when travel to the Holy Land was a popular thing for Americans and Europeans to do.

"With the advent of halftone printing, invented by Frederic Eugene Ives in 1880, images were now becoming more accessible to the public via printed matter—books, magazines, and newspapers—where they were now reproduced alongside text," noted Tom Powers in his 2009 study *Jerusalem's American Colony and Its Photographic Legacy*. Before then, photographs could only be pasted into books by hand as individual prints.[13,14]

A third factor was getting off to a good start, thanks to plain luck.

The first sizeable project of the American Colony documentarians was the newsworthy 1898 state visit of Imperial Germany's Kaiser Wilhelm II and Empress Augusta Victoria to the Holy Land.[15]

Photographers from Jerusalem's American Colony were busy documenting the 1898 visit of Germany's Kaiser Wilhelm II.

The Stars and Stripes was first flown in Jerusalem in 1844. Seen here is the historic US Consulate on Agron Street in downtown Jerusalem.

CHAPTER 3
Visionaries and Crazy People

First US Consul in Jerusalem—A Flamboyant Eccentric Who Made Legal History

In 1844 Philadelphia, Pennsylvania Quaker, Warder Cresson (1798–1860) disembarked at Jaffa to assume his duties as the United States' first Consul in Jerusalem. Eccentric and unstable, it was clear even before Cresson arrived that he wasn't the man for the job. Even though his appointment was rescinded while he was still en route across the Atlantic, Cresson continued to represent himself as US Consul in Jerusalem for four years. During that time, he decided he liked Judaism. Taking the Hebrew name Michael Boaz Israel, he divorced his wife and converted.[1]

Returning to Philadelphia, his ex-wife and children sought to have him declared insane. Cresson appealed the court judgment, arguing that one who changes his religion should not be regarded as crazy, and that the constitution guarantees all Americans are free to practice any religion they wish. He won the case.

The position of Consul in Jerusalem, meanwhile, remained vacant for the next thirteen years until 1857. Cresson, or Boaz as he preferred to be known, returned to Jerusalem. Buried on the Mount of Olives, he was the subject of an exhibit in 2013 at Israel's National Library in Jerusalem. That year, as a result of the initiative to map all the Jewish graves in the vast Mount of Olives Cemetery, Boaz's long-lost headstone was found.

CHAPTER 3

Judah Magnes—A New University for a New Land

While many Christian Americans were swept up in the nineteenth century craze for the Holy Land, some Jewish Americans also supported Zionism. Among them was San Francisco, California-born Rabbi Judah Leon Magnes (1877–1948), who in 1925 became the first chancellor of the newly established Hebrew University of Jerusalem on Mount Scopus.[2]

A pacifist during World War I, Magnes continued his idealist work after settling in Palestine. Together with the renowned German-Jewish religious philosopher Martin Buber, Magnes founded Iḥud (Unity), an association dedicated to the advancement of Arab–Jewish reconciliation. He advocated an Arab–Jewish state that would be part of an Arab Federation. But Magnes' vision of peace never took off. Broken-hearted by the April 13, 1948 massacre of sixty-eight doctors and nurses who were on their way to Hadassah Hospital (next to Hebrew University atop Mount Scopus), Magnes returned to the United States where he died shortly thereafter.

Dr. Archibald C. Harte—Linking the Empire State Building and Jerusalem's YMCA

Dr. Archibald Clinton Harte, a monocle-sporting Southern gentleman from Mobile, Alabama (1865–1946), was part of the American missionary tradition. He dedicated his life to the Young Men's Christian Association (YMCA) that then focused its services on orphaned and poor young men and boys as a means of spreading Christianity.[3]

Having established branches in Ceylon (today Sri Lanka), Burma (today Myanmar), and India, Harte was working at Springfield College in Massachusetts. In 1920 Harte was called to Palestine (which had just been liberated from four centuries of Turkish rule) to serve as the Jerusalem YMCA's general secretary.

The opening of Hebrew University of Jerusalem in 1925: From left: Lord Balfour, High Commissioner Herbert Samuel, Chancellor of Hebrew University Judah L. Magnes, and Zionist leader Chaim Weizmann.

Jerusalem's YMCA, designed by American architect Arthur Loomis Harmon—who had designed the Empire State Building in New York City, remains a landmark in central Jerusalem.

America's Lost Colonies in the Holy Land

At the outbreak of World War I in 1914, the Ottoman authorities banned the YMCA as a suspect organization because it had been founded in London, England. With British military and later civilian rule beginning in 1917, the reopened Jerusalem YMCA flourished. Harte greatly expanded the center's activities, creating an ecumenical meeting place for Jews, Christians, and Muslims. The result of his work so impressed James Newbegin Jarvie, of Montclair, New Jersey that on Christmas Eve 1924, the coffee and sugar importer turned philanthropist pledged one million dollars to build a permanent home for the ever-expanding Jerusalem YMCA.[4]

For Harte who had a penchant for rubbing shoulders with maharajahs and tycoons, only architect Arthur Loomis Harmon (who had designed the one hundred and three story Empire State Building in New York City) could design the Jerusalem International YMCA—a building that the Palestine-based eccentric envisioned as the most beautiful Y in the world.

Motivated by grandeur, Harte kept adding new components to the project (a concert hall and swimming pool), even as the budget soared. Completed in 1933, the neo-Byzantine (ornate style of architecture) stone building, with its elegant arches, domes, and soaring 152-foot-high carillon tower and observation deck, became an instant landmark.

But Harte the spendthrift had fallen out of favor with the YMCA's international board. Arguing over who would control the endowment fund, he resigned and retired to Lake Kinneret, where he passed away in 1946. He bequeathed his home, called Peniel-by-the-Sea since Harte claimed to have seen God's face there, to the Jerusalem YMCA. Today the facility, still run by the YMCA, remains one of Israel's most beautiful inns.[5]

RABBI SHLOMO CARLEBACH

Born in Berlin, Germany to a distinguished line of rabbis, Shlomo Carlebach (1925–1994) escaped the Nazis by fleeing to Vienna, Austria before finding refuge in America in 1939. Ordained as a rabbi by the Lakewood Yeshiva (Orthodox Jewish school) in New Jersey, he was a Jewish free spirit in the 1960s running a commune-like synagogue called the House of Love and Prayer in San Francisco's Haight-Ashbury hippie district. There he added his voice of shalom to the calls for peace.[6]

Reaching out to a generation of alienated youth whose parents or grandparents had discarded Jewish culture, Rabbi Carlebach offered an alternative between the poles of strict Judaism and nonreligious things.

A charismatic musician and performer, the long haired, grey-bearded Carlebach electrified audiences with his mystical stories of Jewish life in eastern Europe before the Holocaust, and soulful music based on biblical verses and Chassidic melodies (extraordinarily pious, mystical music founded in Poland about 1750) and teachings. He composed hundreds of popular tunes putting Psalms to music, which have become mainstays in synagogue rituals and worship, and at wedding and bar mitzvah (Jewish admission ceremony welcoming thirteen year old boys to Judaism) celebrations.

The guitar-toting rabbi brought Jews back to their heritage. In 1976, he established the village of Mevo Modi'in between Tel Aviv and Jerusalem, where two hundred of his American New Age followers moved. Like the settlers of George Jones Adams's American Colony in Jaffa a century before, Carlebach's hippie followers were ill prepared for pioneering in the Middle East. They opened a granola factory, the first in Israel, but lacked the business knowledge to operate it profitably.

Even after his death Carlebach remains a pillar of Israel's new-religious culture, popular with American *ba'al teshuva* (penitent) Jews, many of them settlers in the contested West Bank (a site that both Jews and Muslims think of as sacred, and that they fight over). It's likely the singing rabbi's legacy of outreach through music will only grow stronger. The annual memorial concert held at Jerusalem's convention center draws thousands of devotees. While many of the musicians knew Carlebach personally and played in his bands that toured the former Soviet Union and the United States, a whole new generation has grown up since Carlebach's death that continue to sing his inspiring songs.[7,8]

Sir Moses Montefiore

Montefiore's Windmill, a beloved Jerusalem landmark, was actually built with money bestowed by Judah Touro of New Orleans.

CHAPTER 4
Philanthropists Who Shaped Israel

Tzedakah means charity in Hebrew. It shares the same letters as the word for justice. Tithing, giving away ten percent of one's assets, is a biblical commandment, and supporting just causes has always been a pillar of Judaism. Not surprisingly then, many American Jews have contributed enormously to Israel.

Judah Touro—Benefactor of Jerusalem's First Neighborhood Outside the Old City

Every tourist to Jerusalem stops to admire Montefiore's Windmill and the adjoining scenic neighborhood of Mishkenot Sha'ananim, built in 1857, which was the first Jewish housing estate outside the cramped Old City's Ottoman walls. While British stockbroker Sir Moses Montefiore gets the credit for the visionary project, the truth is that it was his friend Judah Touro of New Orleans (1775–1854) who gifted the money.[1,2,3]

Touro who was a successful merchant, and who gave away a lot of money to different causes, has "the book of Philanthropy, to be remembered forever" inscribed on his tombstone.[4]

In America Touro is remembered for his boundless generosity for such varied causes as the American Revolutionary War monument at Bunker Hill in Boston, Massachusetts and the Touro Infirmary in New Orleans, which became the largest free hospital in Louisiana. But in Israel he is all but forgotten.

CHAPTER 4

Nathan Straus—Dodging the Sinking of the *Titanic* Thanks to his Charity Work

Another all but forgotten benefactor was German-born Nathan Straus (1848–1931), the owner of Macy's department store in Manhattan with his brother Isador. In 1892, as their business prospered, Nathan and his wife Lina funded the Nathan Straus Pasteurized Milk Laboratory to provide bacteria-free milk to American children to combat infant mortality and tuberculosis.[5,6]

Nathan Straus

Nathan Straus's 1912 visit to Palestine affected him profoundly. Nathan and Lina planned to join Isador and his wife Ida on the maiden voyage of the *Titanic* sailing from Southampton, England to New York, but Nathan was delayed by a conference on tuberculosis in Rome, Italy where he was a delegate.

As depicted in James Cameron's blockbuster movie *Titanic*, Ida refused to leave her husband on the sinking ship and get into a rowboat. They drowned together when the ocean liner sank. Feeling he had been spared by divine intervention, Nathan devoted two-thirds of his fortune to helping Palestine. He established a domestic science school for girls in 1912, a health bureau to fight malaria and trachoma, a free public kitchen, and child-health welfare clinics in Jerusalem and Tel Aviv.

Ironically the newly established city of Netanya, founded in 1927, was named in Nathan's honor but the benefactor never gave the municipality a dime.

HENRIETTA SZOLD—FOUNDER OF THE HADASSAH WOMEN'S ORGANIZATION

Baltimore, Maryland-born Henrietta Szold (1860–1945) was both an ardent Zionist and a forerunner of Jewish women's liberation.

In 1909 she traveled to Palestine and was appalled by the starvation and disease she witnessed. Upon her return to the US, she soon founded Hadassah—The Women's Zionist Organization of America, which was (and still is) dedicated to the health, education, and welfare of the Jews and Arabs in Israel.

Her new organization's first mission was to send two American nurses to Palestine to provide pasteurized milk to infants and new mothers, and to permanently destroy trachoma, an easily cured eye disease that was robbing thousands of sight.

By 1918 the Turks had been driven out of Palestine, and Hadassah sent an entire medical unit, composed of forty-five doctors, nurses, dentists and sanitary workers, to bring American-style medical care to serve all, regardless of creed or ethnicity.

During the 1930s Szold involved Hadassah in a program to rescue persecuted Jewish youth from Nazi Germany. It is estimated that the "Youth Aliyah" program she created saved some twenty-two thousand Jewish children from Hitler's concentration camps—and certain death.

Today Hadassah runs two hospitals in Jerusalem, a college, and an abundance of other good works. The women's organization Szold founded now has three hundred thousand members worldwide.[7]

Henrietta Szold in her home in Jerusalem, 1922

Former Israeli Prime Minister Golda Meir

CHAPTER 5
Politicians and Spies

Golda Meir—Israel's Prime Minister from Milwaukee

The US constitution restricts the office of president to native-born sons and daughters. But most countries have no such place-of-birth requirements. Golda Meir, born in 1898 in Kiev, then in Imperial Russia but today the capital of Ukraine, would have been ineligible to become the president of the United States, but from 1969 to 1974 she served as Israel's fourth Prime Minister—after first growing up in Milwaukee, Wisconsin.[1,2]

In Kiev, Golda née Mabovitch witnessed her father boarding up the windows to defend their home from a pogrom (a government-sponsored riot directed against Jews). Arriving penniless in America in 1906, she experienced the hardships many immigrants shared. Even though she didn't know English, she enrolled at Milwaukee's Fourth Street Grade School, today renamed Golda Meir School. When she graduated she was the class valedictorian.

Golda's parents wanted their precocious daughter to marry young but she had other ideas. She ran away to join her sister Sheyna Korngold in Denver, Colorado. The Korngolds' home was the frequent setting for parlor meetings about revolutionary ideas including women's suffrage, workers' unions, and Zionism. The meetings made an impression on teenage Golda. There, she met a sign painter named Morris Meyerson who shared her enthusiasm for the Jewish people's return to Palestine.

CHAPTER 5

Married in 1917, the couple settled at Kibbutz (a communal settlement) Merhavia in the Jezreel Valley. There, Golda planted trees, worked in the chicken coops, and ran the communal kitchen. But it was politics rather than pioneering that drew her. Leaving the kibbutz, the Meyersons (they only changed their surname to the more Hebrew name of Meir after Israel's independence in 1948) moved to Jerusalem. Golda moved quickly up the political ranks, and during World War II she held key posts in the World Zionist Organization and the Jewish Agency, which functioned as the shadow government of the *Yishuv* (Jewish community in British-administered Palestine).

Just before the British quit Palestine, and Israel declared independence, Golda disguised herself as an Arab matron and went to Amman, Transjordan (today Jordan) to secretly meet with Emir Abdullah at his palace. She urged him not to join the other Arab countries in attacking the about-to-be-born Jewish state. Abdullah asked her not to hurry to proclaim statehood. Golda replied, "We've been waiting for two thousand years. Is that hurrying?"

Her proudest moment came in January 1948 when David Ben-Gurion sent her to America with an empty suitcase to raise money to purchase surplus World War II arms for the war they both knew was coming. Golda returned with fifty million dollars. Greeting her at Lydda Aerodrome (today Ben-Gurion International Airport), Ben-Gurion said, "The day when history is written, it will be recorded that it was thanks to a Jewish woman that the Jewish state was born."

Appointed Israel's first Ambassador to the Union of Soviet Socialist Republics (USSR), Golda's presence at Moscow's Great Synagogue on *Rosh Hashana* (Jewish New Year) in September 1948 triggered a spontaneous mass demonstration of Jews who turned out to greet her in defiance of the NKVD (translated as the People's Commissarat for Internal Affairs—or security and law enforcement) secret police.

But Golda's difficult role as a woman in the macho world of generals and intelligence chiefs was ultimately her undoing. In October 1973 on the eve of Yom Kippur (the holiest Jewish holiday, observed by fasting and prayer), Prime Minister Meir received warning that the Egyptian and Syrian armies were about to launch a joint surprise attack. Fearing Israel would lose American military support if she launched a preemptive strike, Meir sat on her hands. It was a tragic error of judgment that cost the lives of 2,521 Israeli soldiers.

While American Jews continued to adore Golda as the iron lady, in Israel she resigned in disgrace. Her vision of peace, framed by her famous remark, "Peace will come when the Arabs love their children more than they hate us," remains unfulfilled.

Golda Meir and John F. Kennedy, December 27, 1962

Golda Meir's grave at Jerusalem's Mount Herzl Cemetery where many national figures are buried

JONATHAN POLLARD—THE SPY WHO EMBARRASSED TWO COUNTRIES

Many countries spy on their enemies. Ditto for their allies. That goes for the good ole US of A; similarly for Israel.

Born in Galveston, Texas in 1954, Jonathan Pollard was no James Bond. But then intelligence and espionage isn't anything like Hollywood movies.[3]

A compulsive liar, ill-suited to keeping state secrets, Pollard slipped between the security cracks to land a job as a Navy intelligence analyst. The Central Intelligence Agency (CIA) rejected him as unsuitable. In 1994, after persuading an Israeli intelligence officer that his offer to provide purloined secrets was not a trick by the Federal Bureau of Investigation (FBI), Pollard began taking paperwork home on the weekends to be photographed by an Israel diplomat, and then returned to work Monday mornings.

Eventually Pollard's erratic work habits raised suspicions. Alerting his wife with their secret code, "Don't forget to water the cactus," the pair hightailed it to the Israeli Embassy in Washington, DC—with the FBI right behind them. Standing at the embassy gates at 3514 International Drive, NW, the Pollards got the shock of their lives. Following the orders of the couple's handler Rafi Eitan, instead of being granted asylum, the guards pulled their guns and ordered the couple to leave. Stepping outside, the Pollards were arrested.

What exactly transpired after that remains a secret. The extent of the damage suffered by the United States is unclear. Jonathan Pollard agreed to a plea bargain. He was given a thirty-year sentence. Belatedly Israel has asked for a presidential pardon—a request that President Barak Obama passed on to Attorney General Eric Holder. Even if no such pardon is granted, Pollard may be released on November 21, 2015 at the end of his term. Or he may die in solitary confinement at North Carolina's Butner Federal Correctional Complex. It is unlikely the details about Pollard's case will emerge soon in one of the most damaging episodes in American-Israeli relations.

Israeli protesters demanding the release of convicted spy Jonathan Pollard

CHAPTER 6
Soldiers, Blockade Runners, and Gun Smugglers

General David "Mickey" Marcus—the Savior of Jerusalem, Shot While Peeing

In 1945 in the aftermath of World War II, the world was awash with surplus weapons. The $50 million raised in America by Golda Meyerson (as she was then called) was used to purchase everything from Spitfire and Messerschmitt-109 warplanes to artillery and boats for the not-yet-born state of Israel and its underground army. But two key problems remained: Britain's Royal Navy continued to blockade the coast until the last day of the Mandate on May 15, 1948, and the Jews of Palestine had relatively few fighters trained in operating heavy weapons.[1]

Ben-Gurion's solution was to call upon veterans of the Allied armies, both Jewish and gentile to volunteer for the fledgling state. About four thousand World War II veterans took up arms for Israel in 1947–1949, and half came from the United States. Some were mercenaries (guns for hire). Most were GIs (former members of the US armed forces) who were shocked to the depths of their souls by what they witnessed when the American army liberated Dachau and other Nazi concentration camps. They vowed "Never again" even as the Arab armies swore to drive the Jews of Israel into the sea.

The highest ranking of the Machal-niks (overseas volunteers) was US Colonel David "Mickey" Marcus, a West Point graduate and D-Day (June 6, 1944) parachute veteran of the invasion of Nazi-occupied France. With Marcus' logistics skills and sheer

CHAPTER 6

Colonel Mickey Marcus

guts, he was appointed Israel's first modern general. He led the campaign to break through to Jerusalem, which had been surrounded and was being attacked. Using pickaxes and shovels to carve out a trail through the mountains to the city (called the Burma Road), Marcus circumvented the Arab *fedayeen* (guerrillas) that had closed the two-lane highway, saving the one hundred thousand Jewish people from starvation.[2]

Terrible things happen in the fog of war. On the eve of June 11, 1948 the United Nations (UN) ordered a ceasefire, and Marcus stepped out of his quarters in the Judean Hills to urinate. A sentry challenged him for the password. Marcus spoke little Hebrew, and responded in English. The guard, mistaking the figure draped in a bed sheet as an enemy infiltrator, shot him.

Hollywood immortalized the friendly fire incident in the 1966 movie *Cast a Giant Shadow* starring Kirk Douglas. The film also gave Michael Douglas his first acting gig.

In 2014 filmmaker Nancy Spielberg (the sister of Steven) released *Above and Beyond: The Birth of the Israeli Air Force*. The eighty-seven-minute documentary tells the story of the American Jewish pilots, barely home from one war, who volunteered to fight in yet another. Those pilots and their fellow Machal-niks (Machal, or Mahal, is the name given to volunteers from abroad) saved Israel from certain destruction.

In Israel, Marcus is remembered differently: In Hebrew slang, Israel Defense Force draftees who don't know how to speak or read Hebrew are sent to a literacy course. What is their name? Marcusim.

SMUGGLED WARPLANES

Not all those post-World War II American overseas volunteers were US Army veterans, and not all fought in Machal. New York City native Murray Greenfield served in the merchant marines. When he heard about the "Aliyah Bet" or "illegal immigration" as the British termed the rescue of Jews who survived the Holocaust (the systematic mass slaughter of European Jews by the Nazis), he joined the American volunteers sailing rust buckets overloaded with refugees—in defiance of the Royal Navy—to take the Holocaust survivors to Palestine. Greenfield's memoirs *The Jews' Secret Fleet: The Untold Story of North American Volunteers Who Smashed the British Blockade of Palestine* documents the brazenness and bravery of the Americans who defied both Great Britain and the FBI.[3]

Among them was William Bernstein of San Francisco, chief mate of the Exodus 1947, who was bludgeoned to death in the wheelhouse when British troops stormed the ship to prevent it from reaching Palestine. The Chesapeake Bay steamer, built in Wilmington, Delaware in 1928 for the Baltimore Steam Packet Company, had been christened the *President Warfield*. She had sailed from Baltimore to Norfolk, Virginia, and seen service in World War II in the Allied Forces' (Britain, France, Russia, and the United States) landing in France. Her last job was to carry 4,554 Holocaust survivors packed aboard a ship meant for six hundred passengers.[4]

Among the other American gunrunners and human smugglers who ran afoul of the FBI, was Adolph (Al) Schwimmer (1917–2011). Putting to good use the experience and contacts he had garnered as an aerospace engineer at Lockheed Martin during World War II, the New York City native smuggled surplus warplanes to Israel. He also recruited the pilots and crews to fly the planes for the brand new Israel Air Force.[5]

Returning to America in 1949, Schwimmer was arrested and convicted for violating the US Neutrality Act. Stripped of his voting rights and veteran benefits, and fined ten thousand dollars, Schwimmer refused to ask for a pardon, believing that smuggling weapons to help create a Jewish State was the right moral decision to make. In 2000, President Bill Clinton pardoned him.

Like Greenfield, Schwimmer ultimately decided to settle in Israel. There, he founded and became the first CEO of Israel Aerospace Industries. The government company today employs more than sixteen thousand engineers and staff, and manufactures both civilian and military aircraft.

Mathematician Robert John Aumann, who splits his time between the State University of New York at Stony Brook and the Hebrew University of Jerusalem, won the Nobel Prize in 2005 for his work on game theory.

CHAPTER 7
SCHOLARS, BRAINIACS, AND ARTISTS—All with an American Accent

Israeli-Americans form a disproportionate share of the brains at Israel's universities, hospitals, and research centers, not to mention in the arts.

Robert John Aumann, a member of the United States National Academy of Sciences, is a good example. A professor at both the State University of New York at Stony Brook and the Hebrew University of Jerusalem, the Frankfurt, Germany-born mathematician won the Nobel Prize in 2005 for his work on game theory.[1]

New York City-born Joseph Cedar is one of Israel's most accomplished filmmakers. His 2007 hit *Beaufort* is about Israel Defense Forces soldiers at a Crusader castle in Lebanon. The film was nominated for an Academy Award in the Best Foreign Film category.[2]

Unique among all these brilliant thinkers and geniuses, was Dr. David Applebaum (1952–2003). The Detroit-born rabbi and physician devoted his life to transforming emergency room medicine in Israel. Not content with the medical care revolution he created at Jerusalem's Shaare Zedek Hospital, he established a chain of emergency care walk-in centers, called Terem, throughout the city.[3]

In New York Applebaum unwittingly delivered his own epitaph, concluding his remarks: "From one moment to the next, we never know what will happen in the ER [emergency room], but it's in Jerusalem that real reality occurs."

CHAPTER 7

Dr. David Appelbaum and his daughter Nava were murdered in the September 9, 2003 Palestinian suicide bombing of the Cafe Hillel in Jerusalem. The attack on the popular restaurant took place the day before Nava was to be married. Dr. Applebaum, the head of the Emergency Room at Jerusalem's Shaarei Zedek Hospital, had treated and saved scores of bombing victims in the past.

On September 9, 2003, having just returned from New York City where he addressed a symposium on terrorism that marked the second anniversary of 9/11, Dr. Applebaum took his twenty-year-old daughter Nava out for coffee on the eve of her wedding. The two were blown to smithereens by a suicide bomber.

WOODSTOCK REVIVAL OFFERS A HEADY MIX OF 1960s NOSTALGIA

If you missed the legendary Woodstock festival at Max Yasgur's Farm at Bethel in upstate New York in August 1969, you can relive the Summer of Love—without the rain and mud—every August in Jerusalem.

The city's Kraft Stadium—a gift from Robert Kraft, the Boston-based owner of the New England Patriots—rocks every summer with a five-hour music marathon. The first rock 'n' roll tribute band festival was held on *Tu b'Av* (the traditional Jewish day of love), August 5, 2009, commemorating forty years since the historic three-day Woodstock Festival.

That benefit concert was organized by the Jerusalem-based not for profit group, American Football in Israel, headquartered at the Kraft Stadium.

The first Jerusalem Woodstock Revival line-up included blues guitarist Ronnie Peterson playing Bob Dylan; singer-guitarist Lazer Lloyd from the rock band Yood with some of Jimi Hendrix's classics; and Eliyahu Sidikman's Crystal Ship tribute band honoring the Doors.

Purists may argue Jim Morrison didn't play at the original Woodstock festival.

"The Doors are set on fire by the band Crystal Ship *in the spirit of Woodstock*," said Carmi Wurtman, the event promoter "because, like The Beatles and a few other world famous bands, The Doors weren't at Woodstock. But they should have been!"

"Max Yasgur's niece Abigail Yasgur, who co-wrote *Max Said Yes* as a tribute to her cousin, Max Yasgur, the hero of the original festival, attended the Jerusalem Woodstock Revival."

"I missed the original Woodstock Festival, and have regretted it ever since," said Kraft Stadium director Steve Leibowitz, who in his other life directs Israel TV's English-language daily news broadcast. "I believe that the music of Woodstock impacted Western culture in a way that no music festival or performer ever has since."

Start planning now for the Woodstock 50th anniversary blow-out in 2019.[4]

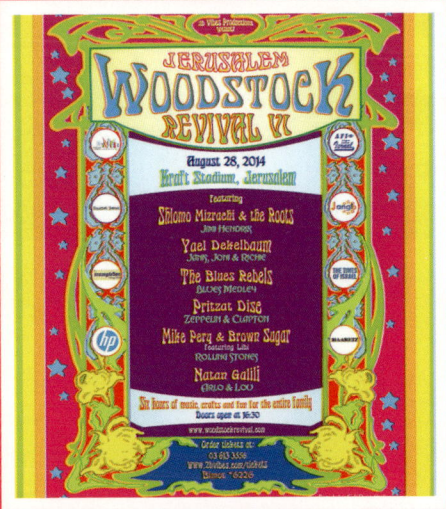

Trenton, New Jersey-born Tal Brody became a superstar for Maccabi Tel Aviv, and made basketball an Israel passion. In 1977, Brody, seen here driving to the hoop for a layup, led Israel to its first European Cup Basketball Championship. Upon beating the heavily favored Soviet Red Army team CSKA Moscow, he famously remarked: *"We are on the map! And we are staying on the map—not only in sports, but in everything."*

CHAPTER 8
Hoopster Coach's Career from Boston to Tel Aviv to Cleveland

Israel can thank Trenton, New Jersey-born Tal Brody (born 1943) for making basketball a national passion in Israel. Picked twelfth in the 1965 National Basketball Association (NBA) draft while playing for the University of Illinois, Brody passed up his NBA career to shoot hoops for the Maccabi Tel Aviv basketball team.[1]

In 1977 at the height of the Cold War, he led the team to its first European Cup Basketball Championship. Along the way, his team defeated the heavily favored Soviet Red Army team CSKA Moscow. Brody's famous remark upon beating the Russians, "We are on the map! And we are staying on the map—not only in sports, but in everything," became a part of Israeli culture. That phrase has been used for decades in various contexts, from political speeches to National Lottery commercials.

Brody trail blazed the hoop dream path for many more Americans coming to the Holy Land. Among them is David Blatt (born 1959) in the Boston suburb of Framingham, Massachusetts. After retiring from basketball as a player, Blatt turned to coaching. Picked as Israel's Coach of the Year four times, Blatt's ultimate triumph in Israel was leading Tel Aviv Maccabi to its sixth Euroleague championship in 2014.[2]

That upset victory led to Blatt being hired as the head coach of the NBA's Cleveland Cavaliers. It was a stunning announcement not just for Israeli hoop fans but also for the

CHAPTER 8

whole country. At a press conference in Tel Aviv, Blatt announced, "I'm leaving my home, but not my family. I'm not necessarily leaving for a better place. I'm leaving to follow my dream."

Blatt made history by becoming the first head coach to move straight from the Euroleague to the NBA without prior playing or coaching experience in a US basketball league. Remarkably in his first season, he led the Cleveland Cavaliers to the NBA finals.

Blatt and Brody symbolize a new reality for Israel. The two thousand-year-old dream of returning to Zion has been achieved thanks in no small measure to the generosity, sweat, and blood of American Jews. Israel, the desolate wasteland that was described a century and a half ago by Mark Twain, has today become an attractive place to live in the global village.

Cleveland Cavaliers head coach David Blatt yells at his team during a pre-season exhibition game against his former team Maccabi Tel Aviv in Cleveland.

BASEBALL IN THE HOLY LAND

The estimated 250,000 Americans living in Israel have brought with them the love of Yankee sports like football, baseball, hockey, and basketball.

In 1986, the Israel Association for Baseball was formed as a non-profit organization for the development and promotion of the sport. The first regulation size hardball diamond was created at Kibbutz Gezer, mid-way between Tel Aviv and Jerusalem. A second field was developed at the Baptist Youth Village near Petach Tikvah, and a third at Tel Aviv's Sportek.

Undaunted by the marketing challenge of establishing a professional league in Israel, Larry Baras, a Brooklyn-born fan of the game and particularly of Dodgers icon Sandy Koufax, who is also Brooklyn-born and Jewish, created the six-team, Israel Baseball League (IBL) in Israel in 2007. Baras signed up Dan Kurtzer, a former US Ambassador to Israel and Egypt and now a professor of Middle East policy studies at Princeton University, to serve as the league's commissioner. Kurtzer threw out the ceremonial first pitch.

But Holy Land hardball is a slightly *meshugana* (crazy) idea that recalls the joke: How do you make a small fortune in Israel? By bringing a big one.

Sandy Koufax

Like the American franchises Dunkin' Donuts, Ben and Jerry's ice cream, and Starbucks coffee, the IBL failed to grow roots in the foreign soil of the Middle East. The league folded after one season.[3,4]

CHAPTER NOTES

Introduction

1. "Palestine 1918 to 1948," *History Learning Site*, 2015, http://www.historylearningsite.co.uk/palestine_1918_to_1948.htm
2. "A Brief History of Yale," *Yale University Library*, http://guides.library.yale.edu/yalehistory
3. Dr. Claire M. Smith, "Overseas Vote Foundation," *OVF Research Newsletter*, Vol. 2, No. 4., August, 2010, 6. https://www.overseasvotefoundation.org/files/counting%20american%20 civilians%20abroad.pdf

Chapter 1. Explorers and Archaeologists

1. Stanley Hoole, ed., "A Visit to the holy Land in 1837," *Journal of the American Oriental Society*, Vol. 95, No. 4, October-December, 1975, University of Alabama, http://www.jstor.org/discover/10.2307/601019?sid=21106008546763&uid=2&uid=3739256&uid=4&uid=3739600
2. "Lowest Elevation: Dead Sea," *Extreme Science*, 2013, http://www.extremescience.com/dead-sea.htm
3. "Map of the River Jordan and Dead Sea: And the Route of the Party Under the Command of Lieutenant W.F. Lynch, United States Navy," *World Digital Library*, July 3, 2013, http://www.wdl.org/en/item/148/
4. "William Francis Lynch (1801–1865), from Jaxton B. Autry, Lynch's Holy Expedition to the Dead Sea and the Surrounding Area," *The Latin Library*, http://www.thelatinlibrary.com/chron/civilwarnotes/lynch.html
5. Naomi Shepherd, *The Zealous Intruders: The Western Discovery of Palestine* (London: William Collins Sons, 1987), 84–89.
6. "Mark Twain in the Holy Land," *Zionism and the State of Israel*, https://zionismandisrael.wordpress.com/2008/08/28/mark-twain-in-the-holy-land/
7. Mark Twain, *The Innocents Abroad* (New York: Signet Classics, 1966), 474.
8. *Institute for Palestine Studies*, No. 50, 23, 2015, http://www.palestine-studies.org/jq/fulltext/78485
9. "Famous Americans Who Made Holy Land Tours," *Bible History Daily*, November 30, 2012, http://www.biblicalarchaeology.org/daily/archaeology-today/biblical-archaeology-topics/famous-americans-who-made-holy-land-tours/
10. "Smith, Eli (1801-1857) American Missionary and Orientalist," *Boston University School of Theology, History of Missiology*, http://www.bu.edu/missiology/missionary-biography/r-s/smith-eli-1801-1857/

CHAPTER NOTES

11. "Holy Land Headliners: A Connecticut Yankee Tackles Biblical Geography," Pilgrimage Panorama, *Gila Yudkin*, 2015, http://www.itsgila.com/headlinersrobinson.htm

12. Wayne Jackson, "Hezekiah's Tunnel," *Christian Courier*, 2015, https://www.christiancourier.com/articles/101-hezekiahs-tunnel

13. "The Construction of Herod's Temple," *Bible History*, http://www.bible-history.com/jewishtemple/Jewish_TempleHerods_temple00000006.htm

14. "Masada." *Unesco.org*, 2015, http://whc.unesco.org/en/list/1040

15. "The President's Address on Presenting Medals," *The Journal of the Royal Geographical Society*, Vol. 12, xi., https://books.google.com

16. Thomas Levy and David Noel Freedman, "William Foxwell Albright," *National Academy of Sciences, Washington, DC. The Bible and Interpretation*, 2015, http://www.bibleinterp.com/articles/albright5.shtml

17. Al Ameer, "Ramallah Friends Schools," 2009, http://www.iro.umontreal.ca/~felipe/IFT6010-Automne2009/Data/TP2/docs/english/r/Ramallah_Friends_Schools

18. "Walworth Barbour American International School in Israel," http://www.wbais.net/page.cfm?p=11

19. "American School of Palestine," http://www.asp.ps/main.php?id=1

20. "University of the Holy Land," http://www.uhl.ac/en/about/uhl-history/

Chapter 2. America's Lost Colonies in the Holy Land

1. "Jaffa Colony Museum," http://www.jaffacolony.com/museum.html

2. Tom Powers, "View From Jerusalem," *WordPress.com*, https://israelpalestineguide.wordpress.com/my-articles/jerusalems-american-colony-and-its-photographic-legacy/

3. "A New England Crusade," *The New England Magazine*, Vol. 36, 201, https://books.google.com/books?id=X_HQQO69g4kC&pg=PA201&dq=George+Jones+Adams+and+the+palestine+emigration+colony

4. Vivian David Lipman, *Americans and the Holy Land through British Eyes, 1820–1917: A Documentary History* (Ann Arbor, MI: University of Michigan, 1989).

5. "The Templers: German Settlers Who Left Their Mark on Palestine," *BBC News Magazine*, July 11, 2013, http://www.bbc.com/news/magazine-22276494

6. "Rolla Floyd," *Find A Grave*, July 2, 2009, http://www.findagrave.com/cgi-bin/fg.cgi?page=gr&GRid=38978321

CHAPTER NOTES

7. "Jerusalem-Tel Aviv Railway Old City Link Planned," *Globes Israel's Business Arena*, October 21, 2013, http://globes.co.il/en/article-10000887581

8. Reed M. Holmes, *The Forerunners: The Tragic Story of 156 Down-East Americans Led to Jaffa in 1866 by Charismatic G.J. Adams to Plant Seeds of Modern Israel* (Independence, MO: Herald Publishing House, 1981).

9. Aviva and Shmuel Bar-Am, "The Sorry Saga of the American Farmers of Jaffa," *The Times of Israel*, March 1, 2014, http://www.timesofisrael.com/the-sorry-saga-of-the-american-farmers-of-jaffa

10. Katherine Cassidy, "Jaffa Expedition Focus of Jonesport Couple," *BDN Maine Archive*, August 11, 2006, http://archive.bangordailynews.com/2006/08/11/jaffa-expedition-focus-of-jonesport-couple/

11. "A Proud History," *The American Colony Hotel Jerusalem*, http://www.americancolony.com/history

12. "The American Colony in Jerusalem, Family Tragedy," and "Onto Jerusalem," *Library of Congress*, http://www.loc.gov/exhibits/americancolony/amcolony-family.html

13. "Halftone Process—Research Article from World of Invention," *Bookrags*, http://www.bookrags.com/research/halftone-process-woi/#gsc.tab=0

14. "Tom Powers—View from Jerusalem: Jerusalem's American Colony and its Photographic Legacy," *WordPress.com*, https://israelpalestineguide.wordpress.com/my-articles/jerusalems-american-colony-and-its-photographic-legacy/

Chapter 3. Visionaries and Meshuganas (Crazy People)

1. "Visit of Kaiser Wilhelm II," *Go Jerusalem*, October 29, 2012, http://www.gojerusalem.com/events/1722/Visit-of-Kaiser-Wilhelm-II/

2. "Warder Cresson (1798-1860)," *Jewish Virtual Library*, 2015, http://www.jewishvirtuallibrary.org/jsource/biography/Cresson.html

3. "Magnes Biography/History," *magnes.org*, http://www.magnes.org/sites/www.magnes.org/files/wjhc1968-030-ar1.pdf

4. "YMCA International Work in Palestine and Israel: An Inventory of its Records," *Kautz Family YMCA Archives, University of Minnesota*, 2005, http://special.lib.umn.edu/findaid/html/ymca/yusa0009x2x2.phtml

5. "A Successful businessman and caring philanthropist," *Jarvie Commonweal Service*, http://www.jarvie.org/about/james-n.-jarvie/

6. "YMCA Peniel-By-Galilee," http://www.ymca-galilee.co.il/about.html

CHAPTER NOTES

7. Shefa Siegel, "Holy Beggars: A Journey from Haight Street to Jerusalem," *Haaretz*, September 4, 2011, http://www.haaretz.com/life/books/shlomo-carlebach-rabbi-of-love-or-undercover-agent-of-orthodox-judaism-1.382475

8. Jodi Rudoren and Isabel Kershner, "Israel to Reopen Contested Holy Site in Jerusalem," *NewYorkTimes.com*, October 30, 2014, http://www.nytimes.com/2014/10/31/world/middleeast/israel-palestinians-jerusalem-temple-mount-al-aksa.html?_r=0

Chapter 4. Philanthropists Who Shaped Israel

1. "Montefiore Windmill," *Travel Jerusalem*, http://www.itraveljerusalem.com/city/jerusalem/montefiore-windmill

2. Jessica Steinberg, "A second wind for Montefiore's magnificent Jerusalem Windmill," *The Times of Israel*, August 31, 2012, http://www.timesofisrael.com/a-second-wind-for-montefiores-magnificent-jerusalem-windmill/l

3. "The Montefiore Windmill," *Jerusalem.com*, April 25, 2013, http://jerusalem.com/articles/travel/the-montefiore-windmill-a2147

4. "Judah Touro (1775–1854)," *Jewish Virtual Library*, http://www.jewishvirtuallibrary.org/jsource/biography/touro.html

5. "The Human Spirit: Storytelling and the 'Titanic,'" *The Jerusalem Post*, http://www.jpost.com/Opinion/Columnists/The-Human-Spirit-Storytelling-and-the-Titanic

6. Naomi Schaefer Riley, "Nathan Straus," *Philanthropy Roundtable*, 2015, http://www.philanthropyroundtable.org/almanac/hall_of_fame/nathan_straus

7. "History," *Hadassah, The Women's Zionist Organization of America, Inc.*, 2015, http://www.hadassah.org/about/history.html

Chapter 5. Politicians and Spies

1. "Golda Meir Biography," *Encyclopedia of World Biography*, http://www.notablebiographies.com/Ma-Mo/Meir-Golda.html

2. "Golda Meir," *Miriam's Cup: Biography*, http://www.miriamscup.com/MeirBiog.htm

Chapter 6. Soldiers, Blockade Runners and Gun Smugglers

1. "British Palestine Mandate: History & Overview (1922–1948)," *Jewish Virtual Library*, http://www.jewishvirtuallibrary.org/jsource/History/mandate3.html

2. David T. Zabecki, "David 'Mickey' Marcus," *History Net*, June 12, 2006, http://www.historynet.com/david-mickey-marcus.htm

CHAPTER NOTES

3. Murray S. Greenfield, *The Jews' Secret Fleet: Untold Story of North American Volunteers Who Smashed the British Blockade* (Jerusalem: Gefen Publishing House, 1999), http://www.amazon.com/The-Jews-Secret-Fleet-Volunteers/dp/9652290238

4. "William (Bill) Bernstein," *World Machal*, http://www.machal.org.il/index.php?option=com_content&view=article&id=300&Itemid=912&lang=en

5. Yossi Melman, "Al Schwimmer, NY-born father of Israel's aerospace industry, dies at 94," *Haaretz*, June 12, 2011, http://www.haaretz.com/print-edition/news/al-schwimmer-ny-born-father-of-israel-s-aerospace-industry-dies-at-94-1.367158

Chapter 7. Scholars, Brainiacs, and Artists—All with an American Accent

1. "Robert J. Aumann—Facts," *Nobelprize.org*, http://www.nobelprize.org/nobel-prizes/economic-sciences/laureates/2005/aumann-facts.html

2. Adi Gold and Raz Shechnik, "Richard Gere to star in Joseph Cedar's new film," *YnetNews.com*, October 12, 2014, http://www.ynetnews.com/articles/0,7340,L-4579744,00.html

3. Greg Myre, "A Healer of Terror Victims Becomes One," *The New York Times*, September 11, 2003, http://www.nytimes.com/2003/09/11/world/a-healer-of-terror-victims-becomes-one.html

4. "Jerusalem Woodstock Revival, August 28, 2014," *Tourist Israel The Guide*, http://www.touristisrael.com/jerusalem-woodstock-revival/688/

Chapter 8. Hoopster Coach's Career from Boston to Tel Aviv to Cleveland

1. Vladimir Stankovic, "Tal Brody, Israeli basketball history," *Euroleague.net*, June 19, 2013, http://www.euroleague.net/features/voices/2012-2013/vladimir-stankovic/i/114392/tal-brody-israeli-basketball-history

2. Danny Chau, "Who's That Guy? New Cavs Coach David Blatt!" *Grantland.com*, June 20, 2014, http://grantland.com/the-triangle/whos-that-guy-david-blatt/

3. William M. Simons, ed., *The Cooperstown Symposium on Baseball and American Culture, 2007–2008* (Jefferson, NC: McFarland Books, 2009), 165.

4. "Kibbutz Gezer Field," *Snipview*, http://www.snipview.com/q/Kibbutz%20Gezer%20Field

WORKS CONSULTED

Avner, Yehuda. *The Prime Ministers: An Intimate Narrative of Israeli Leadership*. Jerusalem: Toby Press, 2010.

Bentwich, Norman. *For Zion's Sake—A Biography of Judah L. Magnes*. Philadelphia: Jewish Publication Society of America, 1954.

Coopersmith, Aryae. *Holy Beggars: A Journey from Haight Street to Jerusalem*. El Granada, CA: One World Lights, 2011.

Feinman, Peter Douglas. *William Foxwell Albright and the Origins of Biblical Archaeology*. Berrien Springs, MI: Andrews University Press, 2004.

Geniesse, Jane Fletcher. *American Priestess: The Extraordinary Story of Anna Spafford and the American Colony in Jerusalem*. New York: Doubleday, 2008.

Greenfield, Murray. *The Jews' Secret Fleet*. Jerusalem: Gefen Publishing, 2010.

Holmes, Reed M. *The ForeRunners*. Independence, MO: Herald Publishing House, 1981.

Holmes, Reed M. *Dreamers of Zion Joseph Smith and George J. Adams: Conviction, Leadership and Israel's Renewal*. Eastbourne, UK: Sussex Academic Press, 2003.

Huhner, Leon. *The Life of Judah Touro (1775–1854)*. Philadelphia: Jewish Publication Society of America, 1946.

Obenzinger, Hilton. *American Palestine: Melville, Twain, and the Holy Land Mania*. Princeton, NJ: Princeton University Press, 1999.

Oren, Michael B. *Power, Faith and Fantasy: America in the Middle East 1776 to the Present*. New York: W.W. Norton, 2007.

Ophir, Nathan. *Rabbi Shlomo Carlebach: Life, Mission, and Legacy*. Jerusalem: Urim, 2014.

Powers, Tom. *Jerusalem's American Colony and Its Photographic Legacy*. 2009. http://israelpalestineguide.wordpress.com/my-articles/jerusalems-american-colony-and-its-photographic-legacy/

Rook, Robert E. *The 150th Anniversary of the United States Expedition to Explore the Dead Sea and the River Jordan*. Amman, Jordan: American Center of Oriental Research, 1998.

Shepherd, Naomi. *The Zealous Intruders: The Western Discovery of Palestine*. London: William Collins Sons, 1987.

Twain, Mark. *The Innocents Abroad*. New York: Signet Classics, 1966.

Vester, Bertha Spafford. *Our Jerusalem: An American Family in the Holy City 1881–1949*. Jerusalem: Ariel, 1988.

Delta Public Library

FURTHER READING

Elkeles, Simone. *How to Ruin a Summer Vacation*. Woodbury, MN: Flux Llewellyn Publications, 2006.
Leibovitz, Liel. *Aliya*. London: St. Martin's Press, 2005.
Singer, Alex. *Alex, Building a Life*. Jerusalem: Gefen Books, 1996.
Uris, Leon. *Exodus*. New York: Bantam, 1983.

ON THE INTERNET

The American School of Palestine
   http://www.asp.ps/
The Walworth Barbour American International School in Israel
   http://www.wbais.net/page.cfm?p=11
Israel Ministry of Foreign Affairs
   http://mfa.gov.il/MFA/IsraelExperience/History/Pages/Archaeological_excavations_Israel_2014.aspx
Jaffa American Colony
   http://www.jaffacolony.com/
The Association of Americans and Canadians in Israel
   http://www.aaci.org.il/

PHOTO CREDITS: Design elements from Thinkstock and Dreamstime/Sharon Beck. Cover, p. 1 (top, left) and p. 52—AP Photo/Mark Duncan; p. 1 (top, right) and p. 35—Center for Jewish History/The Commons; p. 1 (bottom, left)—Library of Congress, (center)—David Rubinger/Time Life Pictures/Getty Images; p. 1 (bottom, right) and p. 46—DMY/Wikimedia Commons; pp. 2, 10 (maps)—United Nations/Public Domain; pp. 2–3 (background), 3–4, 7—Thinkstock; p. 8—Avishai Teicher/Public Domain; p. 10 (inset) and p. 64—Gil Zohar; pp. 11, 34—Public Domain; pp. 12, 14, 16, 18–19, 20 (top), 22, 23, 27, 36—Library of Congress; p. 13—Felix Bensman/Dreamstime; p. 15—Walworth Barbour American International School; p. 20 (bottom)—Avishai Teicher/cc-by-sa 4.0; p. 21—Tamarah/cc-by-sa 2.5; p. 24—Magister/cc-by-sa 3.0; p. 28—Alexey Stiop/Dreamstime; p. 30—Dave Buresh/The Denver Post via Getty Image; p. 32 (background)—Rostislav Ageev/Dreamstime, (inset)—Public Domain; p. 39—US Government/Public Domain; p. 40—Reuvenk/Public Domain; p. 41—Gali Tibbon/AFP/Getty Images; p. 42—Playmount Productions with Katahdin Productions; p. 44—Public Domain; p. 48—Family Photograph/EPA/Newscom; p. 50—Sa'ar Ya'acov/cc-by-sa 3.0, (inset)—Epeefleche1/cc-by-sa 3.0; p. 53—Publicity Still/Public Domain.

GLOSSARY

assassinate (uh-SAS-si-neyt)—to kill suddenly or secretively, especially a politician

chancellor (CHAN-se-lar)—the chief administrative officer in some universities, chief minister of state in some parliamentary governments

charismatic (KAR-iz-MAT-ik)—having charisma, a personal quality that makes an individual attractive or interesting to others

cholera (KOL-er-uh)—an acute, infectious disease characterized by profuse diarrhea, vomiting, cramps, etc.

circumvent (SUR-kum-vent)—to go around or bypass

clapboard (KLAB-erd)—a long, thin wooden board, thicker along one edge than the other, used in covering the outer walls of buildings, chiefly in the Northeastern US

commune (KOM-yoon)—small group of people living together and sharing possessions, work, and income

destitution (DES-ti-TOO-shun)—lacking the means to support oneself, utter poverty

dilapidated (dih-LAP-i-daa-tid)—to fall into a state of disrepair, as by misuse or neglect

disembark (DIS-em-bark)—to leave or unload a ship or airplane

dispersion (dis-PUR-zhen)—to be scattered in different directions or places

disproportionate (DIS-pro-POR-shuh-nit)—out of proportion, in size or number

ecumenical (EK-yoo-MEN-i-kel)—universal; worldwide; promoting Christian unity throughout the world

Euroleague (YUR-o-leeg)—European Basketball League. Because of the Arab boycott, Israeli teams don't compete in Middle Eastern sports leagues

evangelical (EE-van-JEL-i-kel)—in keeping with the Gospels

expatriate (eks-PEY-tree-at)—to send into or become an exile

galvanize (GAL-va-NIYZ) to coat metal, especially iron or steel, with zinc

kaiser (KAHY-zer)—a German emperor, title used 1871–1918

kibbutz (ki-BOOTZ)—a collective agricultural settlement in Israel

maharajah (MA-ha-RAH-ja)—formerly a ruling prince in India

GLOSSARY

Mandate (MAN-dayt)—a commission given by the League of Nations to a member nation to administer a former Turkish territory or German colony. The League of Nations appointed Great Britain to see to the well being of Palestine in 1922 (called the Mandate of Palestine). The end of the Mandate was to "take effect on May 15, 1948. On May 14, 1948, the State of Israel was proclaimed."

missionary (MIS-shu-NER-ee)—a person sent by a church into an area to carry on religious or humanitarian work

NKVD—translated as the People's Commissarat for Internal Affairs—or security and law enforcement; the secret police

orientalism (OR-ee-EN-tl-iz-um)—a trait, custom, or habit of expression characteristic of oriental peoples; learning in oriental subjects

paradox (PARE-e-DOKS)—a seemingly self-contradictory or absurd statement that expresses a possible truth

precocious (pree-KOH-shus)—unusually advanced in mental development

preemptive (pree-EMP-tiv)—to do, acquire, or appropriate before someone else can

purloin (per-LOIN)—to steal or take dishonestly

reconciliation (REK-on-SIL-ee-EY-shun)—the process of reconciling or bringing together divided parties

rescind (ree-SIND)—to repeal, abolish, cancel

trachoma (truh-KOH-muh)—a contagious infection of the eyes that begins with itching, and then blurred vision; left untreated, it can cause blindness

tuberculosis (too-BER-kyoo-LOH-sis)—an infectious disease in the lungs, often fatal

typology (ty-POL-uh-jee)—a systematic classification or study of types

Utopian (yoo-TOH-pee-an)—a visionary system of political or social perfection, an ideal place

valedictorian (VAL-i-dik-TOR-ee-en)—the highest-ranking student in a school graduating class who delivers a speech at graduation

Zionism (ZY-on-izm)—Jewish movement for the establishment and development of the state of Israel

INDEX

Adams, George Jones 16–19, 31
Albright, William Foxwell 14
American Colony Jaffa 17–19, 21
American Colony Jerusalem 17, 22, 23
American Colony Tel Aviv 17
American School of Oriental Research 14
American School of Palestine 15
Applebaum, David 47–48
Aumann, Robert John 46, 47
Bernstein, William 45
Blatt, David 51, 52
Brody, Tal 50, 51, 52
Buber, Martin 26
Carlebach, Shlomo 30, 31
Carter, Jean 20, 21
Cass, Lewis 8, 9
Cresson, Warder 25
Dead Sea 8, 9, 14
Dead Sea Scrolls 14
Floyd, Rolla 19, 20
Grant, Ulysses S. 12
Greenfield, Murray 45
Hadassah Women's Zionist Organization 35
Harmon, Arthur Loomis 28–29
Harte, Archibald 26
Hebrew University of Jerusalem 27
Hezekiah's Tunnel 13
Holmes, Reed 20, 21
Israel Baseball League 53
Ives, Frederic Eugene 23
Jaffa 8–9, 16–23, 25, 31
Jarvie, James Newbegin 29
Jonesport, Maine 21
Jordan River 8–10
Lake Kinneret 9
Lynch, William Francis 9, 11
Magnes, Judah Leon 26–27
Marcus, Mickey 43–44
Meir, Golda 36, 37–40
Melville, Hermann 11
Modi'in, Mevo 31
Montefiore, Moses 32, 33
Nellie Chapin 17, 20
Palestine 6, 9, 11–15, 17, 19, 26, 29, 34–35, 37–38, 43, 45
Pasteurized Milk Laboratory 34
Pollard, Jonathan 41
Powers, Tom 23
President Warfield 45
Robinson, Edward 12–14
Robinson's Arch 13
Schwimmer, Al 45
Smith, Eli 12, 14
Spielberg, Nancy 44
Straus, Nathan 34
Swift, Sara J. 15
Szold, Henrietta 35
Titanic 34
Touro, Judah 32, 33
Twain, Mark 11, 12, 52
University of the Holy Land 15
US Consul 24, 25
USS *Constitution* 8, 9
Walworth Barbour American International School 15
Wilhelm, Kaiser II 23
Woodstock Revival 49
Yale University 6
YMCA 26, 28–29

About the Author

Gil Zohar was born in Toronto, Canada and moved to Jerusalem in 1982. He is a journalist writing for *The Jerusalem Post, Segula* magazine, and other publications. He is also a professional tour guide who likes to weave together the Holy Land's multiple narratives. Zohar wrote one hundred pages of *Fodor's Guide to Israel* (7th edition, 2009) and he has written promotional material for Israel's Ministry of Tourism.